T0199173

THE FATHER'S LOVE

INSPIRATIONAL POEMS

Nancy Carmadelle

Copyright © 2020 by Nancy Carmadelle. 808997

All rights reserved. No part of this book may be
reproduced or transmitted in any form or by any means,
electronic or mechanical, including photocopying,
recording, or by any information storage and retrieval
system, without permission in writing from the copyright
owner.

To order additional copies of this book, contact:
Xlibris
1-888-795-4274
www.Xlibris.com
Orders@Xlibris.com

ISBN: Softcover   978-1-7960-8775-8
         EBook   978-1-7960-8776-5

Print information available on the last page

Rev. date: 02/12/2020

A Ray of Sunlight

The sun peaks through the darkness, a new day Is born, leaving the night behind behold a new dawn.
When the flowers and leaves are touched by his rays, they seem to reach up in a hallelujah praise.
When the dance is over between earth and sun, day gives away to night and a new cycle is begun.
A heavenly gift that keeps giving, to one to all, its glory never fails; never falls

A Dream

What a lovely night we had together talking, laughing sharing a meal with you seeing the smile upon your beautiful face only to awake from a distant place.
A sweet dream it was where time has no measure, memories from my heart of life's past pleasure.
One day we'll gather on Heaven's Shore where nothing will part us forever more.
We'll laugh and have a dance or two and celebrate the Lord. As we all sing in cue.

A Saviour's Journey

If I were there when your journey begun what amazing things I would hear, as your precious words rings truth to my ear.

To the lame you said walk to the blind you said see how the dead did rise from a command by thee.

My heart would be humbled I would learn to pray as I watch each miracle you performed along the way.

I would listen to your stories in your still small voice granting me privileges; granting me a choice.

How difficult it would be at your journeys end when at the cross you would die for my sin.

Day turns to darkness as your light departs the earth and all those who will love you shall have a new birth.

LIFE

Enjoy life's journey traveled under the moon and sun each day a new beginning that just begun.
There will be challenges many to be sure tribulation always at the door.
Greet them with a smile and courage of heart for victory is yours right from the start.
don't fear what tomorrow brings; yesterday is gone, live in today's moment as time passes on.
Remember the gift of life will reach its journeys end for time has its limits to all therein.

HAPPY BIRTHDAY

Today is a very special day the anniversary of your birth this day the good lord blessed you with life here on earth.

I hope you laugh till you cry and dance the day away open gifts many or few given in love just especially for you.

Share your day with those near to your heart celebrating with them as this day finally departs.

So Happy birthday to you let the party begin let's celebrate this day til the very end.

MASTER POTTER

Place me master potter within your gentle hands use all your talent and skill of art fill this vessel with the spirit of your heart.

Created from mother earth by your design formed to your image, beauty and mind.

Like a skillful potter with his polishing stone work out my imperfections never leaving me alone.

Pray over this vessel as you work with your hands that all my impurities I come to understand.

This vessel now complete and ready to share the love of the creator to everyone; everywhere.

BEAUTIFUL DAY

What a beautiful day I awoke to behold not knowing what good things today would unfold.
As I watch the sun peaking through the sky the beauty of its sight just captured my eye.
I hear the birds singing so sweet a song calling for a mate he hopes will come along.
I See the flowers in their bloom scattered like a painted scene releasing its aroma its scent quite serene.

My Mom

Mom you're special I must say raising me was not easy but you done it in such a loving way.
Your touch was so gentle as you embrace me with love warming my heart like a ray from above.
Each day you cooked and cleaned your work never done so I could run and play under the sun.
Your voice calming to my very soul rings in truth even now that I am old.
You didn't love me just now and then but with the kind of love that has no end.
To sum it all up I never could I owe you a life time of so much good.

PRAYER

You hear from Heaven your dwelling place every prayer I ever told by the power of prayer I find you there lover of my soul.

Lord Jesus I seek your holy face that I might stand in your amazing grace.

May the incense of my prayers enter the alter of your heart bestowing your protection each day I embark.

I find fulness of joy in your presence alone as I bow before your throne.

It's there I leave this troubled world and all it can afford so with a faithful heart I can now depart to find them never more.

SISTER

If I could write a poem it would be like this because you're the best sister that could ever exist.
When you saw me cry you got up and held my hand so much love I could scarcely understand.
We laughed; we talked the whole day through we share everything even the flu.
I'm so happy when you're around joking and laughing just playing the clown.
Seriously sister I thank God for you and I want you to know that I love you too.

SERVING KING

My story is about you, it's very old but ever true, a servant king you came to be, a Lord, a Christ to me. You walked the long and painful path all the way to Calvary you cast down your crown left heaven above just to show your amazing love.

You are the salt of the Earth, a light unto the lost beauty for ashes who can know your cost the blood you shed was not in vain for my life ever bears your stain.

INFINITE LOVE

You sit in the seat of emotions will and thought your love abides there with me in your heart.

With infinite love you embrace me, the grandeur of it all, a Saviour you became to recover my fall.

You keep no records of my many wrongs done within your very sight or the countless times I've failed you in the dept of the night.

I'm never unnoticed never unseen in the essence of Your love never have You failed me or ever faltered placing me always before your holy alter.

I will rejoice not in a boastful pride, but in your truth that sets me free how impossible for You to fail me is my reality.

Printed in the United States
By Bookmasters